IN THE NOTE OF C

BY CHERYL S. SMITH

1stBooks - rev. 12/17/01

ACKNOWLEDGEMENTS

There are far too many people to thank individually for the success of this book, but you know who you are. I would be remiss if I did not send hallelujahs and praise to the Almighty -God is my source and my supply. Of course there are those who deserve special mention - Maritza Pinto, Sharon Beauregard, Angela Henderson, Reggie Price, Angelena Kellum, Rosalind Davis, Kent O'Neal, Maria Rubalcava, Brian Carlson, Gregory Banks, Aroldo Flores, Toni Scott-Cohn, TeSaxton Sarwar, Lesle Smith, Solomon Smith III and my father Solomon Smith Jr. All you have forgiven me and encouraged me throughout my "mad artist" stage. A special thank you goes out to my aunts 'MaMa' Milawne McBride, 'Auntie AA' Ava Brown, and my loving mother Chanita Smith-Williamson. Without your motherly nurturing, wit and wisdom I would not have been strong enough to become as successful as I am. An honorable mention goes to Jeremiah McAllister for photographing a challenging subject and producing an attractive product. A special shout out to my daughter's godparents, Michael Smith and Gina 'GiGi" McAllister. Both of you have been there for an awfully long time and continually ensure my mental wellness. Lastly, a big ole' loving hug to all of the fellas in my distant, and not so distant, past who showed me each and every time that I deserved more.

Keep shining yall' & until next trip be blessed and travel safely with the Divine.

DEDICATIONS

This book is dedicated to my beautiful daughter Amira Milawne. She is **the** most wonderful gift that has come into my life. Throughout my pregnancy, her infancy and prayerfully for the rest of my life she is constantly teaching me new and magnificent lessons about life. God is clearly seen in and through the eyes of children.

TABLE OF CONTENTS

INTRODUCTION

How does one introduce an introduction? The short story and poems to follow are a sort of written photo-album of my life over the last 10 years. Since this is my first published book, I view this collection of writings an introduction of my life's drama - my observations, work, play, love, passion, joy, and disappointments - to the world. Within these pages you will take a walk down my memory lane. Not all of my experiences have been painless, but is that not true for every human being? Despite the challenges that may have come my way, I must attest to being exceedingly blessed.

The short story, Something Happened Really, deals with date rape and is autobiographical in nature. The names and places have been changed or omitted to protect the innocent and not so innocent. It has taken me eight years of my life to "deal with" this experience. Part of my healing process was that I had to admit that something damaging, life altering and violent happened to me. It has only been within the last two years that I have been able to talk about the subject of rape and that I have been a victim. I was not just a victim of the crime of rape, but in some ways a victim of my own silence and more accurately my denial. My refusal to confront my assailant and my subsequent refusal to confront my "issues" stifled my spirit. My spirit that permitted me to live a healthy, whole and joyful life was all but dead. I was so busy pushing down the hurt, anger, despair, and confusion that I all but smothered the positive in my soul. Once I started to let go of the negative in my life, I was able to live - truly live. A great part of my living is writing. This book is a product of that process.

If there is one single thing that I want the readers of this book to walk away with is the fact that no one, male or female, is responsible for their own victimization or being abused. The most damaging choice I made 10 years ago was that of being silent. Tell someone - the police, a doctor, a friend, clergy, an adult, and/or a counselor - of your experience past or present! Additionally, just because you have been a victim does not mean you have to spend your entire life in that state. We have choices in almost every life situation. We can choose to move onward and upward. Admittedly, I still battle with my own demons. It is not easy, but it is not impossible.

I wish you success in attaining peace, joy and bountiful blessings!

Your Sista' in Love,

Cheryl S.

xi

SECTION I -

SOMETHING HAPPENED

CHERYL S. SMITH

<u>Something Happened, Really</u>

"Girl, what time is it?" I had been on the phone with Denise for a 1/2 hour catching up on her latest life's drama. I was half-assed listening while searching my closet and applying my make-up for my date. What I had gathered was that she and her current man had just got into it about her 6 year-old son's behavior. He was bad as hell. I could never tell her that though, because he was an absolute angel in her eyes. If the truth were told he was hell on a big wheel.

"It is 7:30. Why? What's up?" She replied.

"I have a date with Richard at 8 and I haven't even started on my hair. Let me let you go." I said as I went to plug in the curling irons. I had just gotten my hair cut into a short layered look like Anita Baker's latest. It was sharp as hell, but a pain to curl.

"Unt uhn, not until you tell me where you are going. I heard he just got a new Bronco his parent's bought him. Why you didn't ask him to hook me up with one of his boyz?" Denise was sweet, but CRAZY. She was always trying to get with a brother for his cash, gear or car. Never mind that most of them were drug dealers or wanna be's. She was definitely what I call a motor head. She knew more about the latest model cars and how much they cost than any man I ever knew.

"He said we would check out one of those Thai restaurants on Broadway. And yes Mz. Thang, he has a new car. How the hell did you know that? He just got it last week, I haven't even seen it."

"Pa-leeze" she said. "You know how small Seattle is. Remember? My sister Tina knows one of his boyz and she told me all about it. So you gon' give him some? This is your third date." She shamelessly asked.

"Denise why you always trying to put me on my back for some dude?" I laughed. "I don't know though, he is kinda sexy, we'll see."

"We'll see my ass!" She teased. "You know you want some. Shit, when was the last time, a few months ago? With ole boy, Mr. Goofy artist. You better give him some. What you wait'n on? If you don't, there are plenty of skeezers who will."

We both laughed. Leave it to Denise to state the obvious.

"Oh shut up heffa'. I gotta go. Love ya!"

I hung up the phone and ran to finish getting dressed.

As I curled my hair I thought about what Denise had said. She had already given me the 411 on Richard. They went to Rainier high school together. He played football, baseball and ran track. He even had good grades to boot. With all that he got the "man" status not to mention his parents were well off. From our first two dates I learned his dad was a doctor and his mom was from old black money. They lived in a home in the CD, Central District, where all the

3

well-to-do's of all colors lived. Seattle was a lot different than Chicago about race. You saw inter-racial couples all the time. It was definitely Jungle Fever City. People of all races lived in the same neighborhoods, their children went to the same schools and they seemed to do it all harmoniously. If you had money, you lived around folks with money and if you were poor, you lived with other po' folks. It was that simple, but it took some getting used to. It wasn't that cut and dry in Chicago. There were very few neighborhoods that were mixed and it most certainly wasn't always so comfortable. Even today, in 1992, there were still some places in Chicago a Black person better not think about slowing down in after dark.

The doorbell rang. I took one last look in the mirror, sprayed on some of my new perfume and blew my reflection a kiss. You go girl! I thought as I went to answer the door.

Richard was wearing a suede black jacket, black turtleneck sweater and tight jeans. All that black made me think of a panther - sexy and dangerous. I had decided on a pale seafoam green sweater and skirt set I had just picked up at a small little trendy shop in Pioneer Square. It was a little bit out of my budget, but I loved the way the green complimented the reddish undertones of my brown skin. When we got to his truck he opened the door for me and helped me climb in. I'm sure he was trying to get a peek up my short skirt. Good thing I had on new tights and not the old ones with the whole in the butt. When he got in he said, "Mmmm, baby what scent you wearing? You smell good."

"Beautiful", I answered.

"Yes you are", he smiled as he pulled off with a screech.

We arrived at the restaurant at about 8:30, just as the dinner crowd had started to thin out. This was one of the most popular Thai restaurants in the city. My aunt and I used to come here for lunch before she moved back home. The hostess informed us there was a short wait. We watched the chefs prepare the other patrons' meals as we waited. The kitchen was set up short order style in the front of the restaurant so everyone had a front row seat to the meals being expertly assembled. We chatted about our week's happenings. He mentioned he was glad that midterms were finally over. Richard was a senior, majoring in Biology, at Seattle University. He had been accepted to a couple of graduate schools but had planned on going to Stanford Medical School. I asked him how his test went.

"Cool, cool, but that damn statistic class is kicking my ass man. I can't wait till this semester is over. I'll have all my prerequisites done and I can kick back and coast through the spring. California here I come!" I smiled because I thought his boyish enthusiasm was really too cute. As he rambled on about one of his professors being boring I began wondering if he and I would continue to see one another after he graduated. I had just started at Seattle Central Community College, and he was well on his way to becoming a doctor like his

4

father. I decided that I probably wouldn't. I was certain that he would find some little cute thing that would keep him busy. My thoughts were interrupted by the hostess telling us to follow her to our table.

"Baby what cha' havin'? And don't take your time about it either. I'm starvin'." We had barely sat down and picked up our menus. It bothers me to be rushed and I hate bossy men. I made a mental note to work on that. At least he didn't insult my intelligence by trying to order for me. I still marveled at how many times I have seen that on TV. As if a woman can't make up her mind about what she wants and that she is so feeble-minded that she needs someone to tell her what she would like to eat. Who the hell thought of that?

We placed our orders. He ordered Kai Pad Khing, a stir fried chicken with ginger dish. I kept to my favorite, Pad Thai with shrimp, a spicy rice noodle dish with peanut sauce. Together we chose the spring rolls for our appetizer. When the food arrived we dug in with both hands and made an attempt at small talk between bites. "You going back to Chi for Thanksgiving?"

"Naa, the tickets are way too expensive for a sista."

"How much you need? I got a few ends in the bank. I know we could work out some sort of payment arrangement."

"Thanks, but I think I'll just go over my girl's house with her family." Just who did he think I was, someone who would sleep with him for a plane ticket? I don't think so!

"Well you could come over and have dinner with me and my family. My sister is flying in from school and I want you to meet her."

I almost choked. First he throws out the have pussy will travel suggestion. Now he wants me to meet the family. Wait till I talk to Denise tomorrow, she'll love that one.

"I'll let you know, but Denise's mom can throw down in the kitchen. I've been looking forward to gettin' some of her greens."

"Well my mama ain't so bad a cook. She is known to burn a few peach cobblers- literally", he said jokingly. Well at least he is funny, I thought as we both laughed at his poke at his mother's cooking. I think I like this guy.

He asked me what I wanted to do next as we were leaving. It was the first week of November but the weather was still pretty warm. I suggested we walk down to SBC, Seattle's Best Coffee, to get a after dinner pick me up. I had only been in Seattle for a little over a year and really didn't have much of an idea about what there was to do in the city, except for coffee. There were coffee stands everywhere you turned in this town. He said we could go back to his place to chill. I was a bit hesitant because his place was actually his parent's. He explained that they had just left for vacation to Bermuda the day before. Since they were gone, it sounded like a plan.

The house was just as I imagined. A huge ranch style home with a heated two-car garage, large pool, and guest house. "It's beautiful," I gushed. "How many bedrooms?"

"There are five bedrooms if you don't count the den that doubles as the guest bedroom." He said, sounding a little annoyed by the question.

"You okay?" I asked as we walked through the backdoor that lead into the kitchen. I hoped I didn't sound like one of those girls who were diggin' him for the money.

"Yeah, I'm straight", he replied, but I could tell something was wrong.

He pulled off his jacket and threw it on a nearby chair. I hung back in the doorway and took a look around the kitchen.

"Come on in, I don't bite" he said over his shoulder as he went to the refrigerator. He pulled out a bottle of wine and grabbed my hand. He led me through the dining room to the living room. I noticed that there were tastefully framed prints on the wall by Ralfie, Lawrence and Lee. The furniture had an expensive look, like something out of Better Homes and Gardens - classy, well laid out and comfortable. I had decided that this was definitely how I wanted my home to look.

"So what do you think?' he asked as he uncorked the wine.

"I'm glad that wine has a cork and not a screw off cap."

"Ah, so you been hanging around riff raff? Get used to it, cuz I can't get with no ghetto bunnies."

For the second time this evening I was insulted. Just what did he think of me? I wondered. I had to set him straight on this one, so I said, "It's not that I am ghetto. Most college guys drink beer and have no taste for wine. And the wine that most of them can afford to drink is cheap."

"I hear you but I don't drink beer. Beer makes you fat, and you know I can't be walking around with a gut. Gotta' keep it tight." He said as he patted his flat abs.

I sat down in one of the two big chairs in the living room. He stretched out on the couch. He reached over and picked up one of three remotes off the coffee table. He pressed a couple of buttons and music seemed to be coming from everywhere. He poured the wine. I picked up my glass and sunk back into the chair. I began to sing along to a Phyllis Hyman tune.

"You have a nice voice", he said.

"Well thank you", I gushed. "I try, but I do a better job at trying than actually singing." I kicked up my feet onto the ottoman and closed my eyes just letting Ms. "Diva Queen" Hyman take me away. I was just finishing my wine when he said, "Why you way over there? Come sit next to me" I opened my eyes and saw that he was patting the space next to him on the couch. I got up, feeling a little uneasy. I knew he would try to kiss me, and that is when I had a flashback of the last time we kissed. It was awful. I remembered thinking I was drowning. I imagined it is what it would be like kissing a St. Bernard - all tongue and saliva.

He wasted no time. He leaned over and covered my mouth with wet sloppy kisses. He moved down to my neck and began to move his hand up my thighs. He moved in closer, pressing his body to mine so I could feel his erection. I squirmed from under his weight. He wasn't having it. He swiftly readjusted, this time pinning me into the corner of the sofa. I pushed at his shoulders and said, "Richard slow down, wait a minute." He ignored me and put his hands up my sweater, quickly undoing my bra. He grabbed my left breast and began to squeeze my nipple. "Ow! Stop, that hurts", I complained. I tried to push him off but he just squeezed harder. "Goddammit Richard stop! You are hurting me!" I yelled.

"Shut the fuck up", he growled.

Oh my God, he is crazy. What am I going to do, I thought as I started to panic. I began to struggle against him. He was too strong and he leaned in harder, pushing himself into me. I had played out similar scenarios before and fought off unwanted advances. I knew instinctively, somehow, this incident was different. It was like he was not really there and no was not something he would hear, no matter how I said it. He pulled back to unbuckle his pants and that is when I pushed him off of me with everything I had. He flew back and I ran in the direction where I thought the front door should be. I didn't know for sure, but I knew I had to get out of there. I got as far as the foyer.

He grabbed me by my hair. I yelled from the pain as he drug me by my hair back down the hall. "Yell louder bitch! Can't nobody hear your fat ass. I'll give your ass something to yell about!" I felt my skirt catch on something and tore. He still had a hand full of my hair as he mounted me. "Richard please stop", I begged. I grabbed his hand to stop him from pulling down my tights and panties. He let go of my hair, grabbed my hand and bent it back until I thought my wrist would break. He grabbed the other hand and put it with the other. I pulled my right hand loose and clawed at his face. He punched me in the face and it felt like I had been hit with a sandbag. He pulled down my panties and forced his fingers into me. "No, no, please stop! Richard what are you doing, please!" I screamed.

"Yeah, I like that. Come on beg me. That's right, keep moving. Beg me for it", he said in a demonic voice. He forced himself into me. A lifetime passed as he pumped. I just laid there, because there was no more need to fight. Inside I begged God for death, which I knew to be my only escape. He withdrew as he climaxed and sprayed semen all over my brand new outfit. He got up and left me laying on the floor. I couldn't move. I tried, but every part of my body was numb. He must have killed me. I couldn't think for what felt like hours. Then I heard him coming and my body made its own movements. I got up on my knees and pulled myself off the floor. I ran back to the front door. He laughed as he followed me. "Where the fuck do you think you are going looking like that? Wash your nasty ass with this", he said as he threw a wet towel at my head. "You are ugly as hell." I just stood there, not thinking, just standing and wondering what to do. All I knew is that I had to get away. I picked up the towel and wiped his cum off of my clothes. "Bring your nasty ass on, I'm taking you home", he sneered. He went back down the hall to the back door. He yelled back, "Bring your ass on before I come in there and beat your fat ass!" My legs felt like they were made of the same wood as the dining room furniture. Through my tears the back door seemed like it was miles away. Wake up Sylvia, Wake up! Is what I kept repeating to myself with every step I took. When I finally made it outside to the car, the passenger side door was open. I saw that he had put my shoes and underwear on the floor. He drove recklessly all the way back to my Rainier Valley apartment. "Get the fuck out!" he yelled when we pulled in front. I wasn't moving fast enough so he slammed my head against the window, and reached across me to open the door. I hit him in the side of the face and began to kick and scream. He withdrew and jumped out the driver's side. I moved quickly to open and exit the truck. He met me on my side, raised his hand to hit me and I cowered away. He grabbed my things out the front and threw them on the curb. He climbed in on the passenger side and pulled off with a screech.

I walked up my long flight of front steps leading from the street to my door. I didn't remember picking up my shoes and purse until I reached the door. When did I get these? I wondered as I unlocked the door. I walked inside, closed the door, locked it and lay on the floor.

I woke the next day to the phone ringing. It was Saturday and I should have been at work. I went to pull myself off the floor and I screamed out. My whole body hurt. This is when I recalled the night before. What happened? I got up and answered the phone. My boss was on the other end. I think he was asking me why I wasn't at work. What was he talking about, I'm dead. Dead people don't work...I heard myself say, "I'm sorry I don't feel well. I need a few days off." I must have sounded convincing because he said, "Call me when you feel better and I will put you back on the schedule."

I undressed and threw my clothes in the trash. I looked at myself in the bathroom mirror. Who is that? Damn you are a mess. My chest and arms were black and purple with bruises and the left side of my face was swollen. Ice, I need ice. I went to the kitchen and pulled out the ice tray with shaking hands. I couldn't stop the shaking so I placed the tray on the counter to gather myself. A towel, I need a towel. I walked to my hall linen closet and found a hand towel. Now go back and put the ice in the towel. What is wrong with you? Think. I poured ice into a hand towel and applied it to my swollen face. When I put it to my face I felt nothing at all. I walked to my bedroom and lay down with my homemade ice pack on my face. I felt so exhausted, and wasn't thinking clearly, I must be sick.

The phone was ringing. Sylvia get up the phone is ringing.

"Hey Syl, where you been? I've been calling your ass for two days."

"Who is this?" I asked.

"What you mean, it's Denise. Where you been?" She demanded.

"I'm here."

"You sound strange. What's wrong with you?

"I just don't feel well."

"Oh, well you need something? I know the weather is a trip, warm one day and then cold and rainy the next. You taking some medicine? I got some alka seltzer plus. Me and little Pete can come over..."

"NO!" I screamed.

"What ya' yelling about. You sure you okay?"

"Yea, I'm all right. Just need some rest. I'll call you back."

"Wait one damn minute. I know you ain't trying to hang up and not tell me about your date. I've been calling you all weekend so I can get the details. You know I live vicariously through you, so spill it. What happened?"

"Nothing." I whispered as tears started streaming down my face.

"Nothing? All come on! Don't be holding back on me," she insisted.

"Nothing happened, really. I have to go."

I rolled over and hugged my body. Everything on the inside of me felt like it was trying to come out through my chest. Eventually the tears stopped and I fell soundly asleep. I woke up to blackness. The daylight came and went and brought in another night. I just lay there for what I thought was an eternity. Finally another morning came and I wondered what day it was. I turned on the TV and the anchorwoman answered that question. It was Tuesday and it was going to rain all day. I got up and showered. Once I finished I started to step out and couldn't. I felt as if I was still covered with dirt so I showered again. I looked down at my body and saw that the bruises were starting to heal. I made myself go to my bedroom closet and picked out something to wear. I got to get to class, I kept thinking. I put on a long sleeve black sweater with a pair of black pants. *Black, like a panther - sexy and dangerous.* I laughed out loud. *Nothing happened, really!* I said to the empty room. I sat on the side of my bed and laughed and cried at the same time. *How is it I still breathe if I am dead?*

Something Happened

Hey you
Face all made up
A painted on expression
A perfect smile.
Yeah you
With the dead eyes
What was your tribulation?
What was your trial?

Tell it, something happened

You can't live the lie
There is no hiding place
Not from self.
No matter how hard you try
You will never win the race
Not from self.

Tell me, something happened

Did he beat you?
Your soul is tarnished,
(Never to shine again)
Did you bleed?
Or was his fetish torture with words?
(It is always about pain)
After, what did you do?
No words of advice to heed.
Do you dream?
Replays of your nightmare in screams.

Tell someone, something happened

Was he someone you trusted?
Your date, a neighbor or your father
Now he is your own personal bogeyman
Your pipe dreams are contaminated & rusted
To trust yourself again is a bother
You think you can't love, but I know you can.

Get help, something happened

That something is rape
& it happened you can't deny
It is a crime against everyone
A crime of hate, with no escape
Calling it lust is a lie
It never goes away, & cannot be undone.

Call the police, something happened

Someone else needs you to tell the story
It is not your sin, let go of the shame
Save your soul, renew spirit, & resurrect your will
Just by facing it you start walking to glory
Release your fear & relinquish your pain
Silence is deadly, the mute can never heal.

Scream! Let it out, SOMETHING HAPPENED!

8/3/01

SECTION II -

POETIC HEALING

IN THE NOTE OF C

"As human beings, our greatness lies not so much in being able to remake the world...as in being able to remake ourselves."

-Mahatma Gandhi

In The Note of C

Writing is my release
Words offer me peace
What is produced is my voice
I feel compelled, I have no choice.

I expose myself in this way
I give life to what I have to say
It does not matter if it is understood
Feel free to interpret bad & good.

We all have different ways we express
What our souls refuse to lie to rest
God gifted me with the art of language
All my words need to be said.

So I write on in my own octave and key
The key that I choose is that of C
Truly they are notes, I'm sure you'll agree
And the C I mention is me.

3/28/01

PRACTICED SCALES OF INSPIRATION

"Do not go where the path may lead, go instead where there is no path and leave a trail."

-Ralph Waldo Emerson

Writing About It

The madness & the beauty that I see
As life passes by me.
Inspires my pen to move
To write about it, is what I choose.

I could cry & wallow
At the atrocities all around.
Or I could stand in awe
At the magnificence abound.

Instead, I do what is natural
I convey my feelings, true & factual.
On this paper for all to share
My words to last forever, always there.

For too long I ignored the call
To do what God has gifted
The ability to tell it all
Perhaps, after it is all said, some are uplifted.

I suppose I will never be certain
Until they drop the curtain.
If my expressions made an impression
On a mind, heart or spirit, given some direction.

To tell a tale or relay a message
I find solace, my voice to speak out.
To a world full of my brethren
Who would like to know what I write about?

8/6/01

Keep on Steppin'

We are all faced with challenges,
& I will share how I deal with mine.
It may seem difficult at first,
But the ease you will find.

I keep on steppin'

I mean high steppin' like a cheerleader,
Head erect, chest out & feelin' strong.
No matter what is the matter,
No matter what has gone wrong.

I keep on steppin'

Sometimes I keep steppin' on like a warrior,
Fighting the good fight until the battle is won.
I may return to my home weary & tattered,
But I am also stronger, & relish in what is done.

I keep on steppin'

Often I step like that of a graceful dancer,
With style & poise I gingerly bound about.
I inspire other leaders to dance with me,
& compel the wall flowers to shout.

I keep on steppin'

I step out into the world ready & prepared,
Equipping myself with God's armor & fire.
I constantly set new goals & master tasks,
Sure to thank Him for His protection before I retire.

I keep on steppin'

So when adversity & the oppressive show up in your life,
I hope you remember my secret as to what you should do.
Don't waste valuable energy on idle & idiotic concerns,
I tell you put one foot in front of the other, this ain't nothin' new.

Keep steppin'

3/27/01

A Talk

Last night I had a talk with my Father
I was wondering why I care for people,
& What was the reason I even bother.

Me: Father why do I care for others
        Why do I try to connect with my sisters and brothers?

G: You do so because you recognize the need
      I gave the gift of compassion, and other souls you try to feed.

Me: But too often I am misunderstood
        I am suspected of trying to do anything but good.

G: You are not understood because the world is full of the blind
      Some of those you encounter don't use their heart, they are directed by
      the mind.

Me: Yeah, I know that we are all in different spaces and mindsets
        But it gets me down that my earth family is not ready yet.
        They seem not to be able to decipher that I mean no harm
        So how do I get through to them? Is it a waste of my charm?

G: Child if you truly understand that all of you are on different pages
      Then it should not be hard to follow the wisdom of the sages.
      Be of good faith and do not fret, nor worry
      Ask yourself what is your hurry?

Me: I feel rushed because I know that tomorrow is not promised to come
        I constantly see the need for love for each and everyone.
        Father is it too much to ask that you show me the way?
        Because I am feeling overwhelmed and to you I pray.

G: Little girl for you I am always available
      You just have to have faith that I am willing and able.
      Tell me what you want and I will make it come to pass
      Fore I make all things possible, all blessing come from me and they
      always have.

Me: I pray that the evil forces won't squash my desire to touch other human
       beings
       And it is also my prayer that this disharmony will not keep me from
       seeing.
       My dreams realized; the dream of true friendship and of unity.
       I pray that my child and her children's children will live happily.

G: Oh, is that all my dearest one, is that all you desire
       Do you ask nothing for yourself?
       Fore you know I AM the provider of all wealth.

Me: Help me walk through life, through all this hell and fire,
       And I pray for your guidance and wisdom
       To help bring to life all the blessings that will come.

G: What you are asking is already being done.
       Most of the battles of life you have already won.
       Keep leaning on me for your strength and your power.
       And I will guide and protect you each and every hour.

I said thank you Lord for all your grace and mercy.
God I know that with you at my side, no weapon can prosper against me.
I will keep on trying, doing the right things in the correct spirit.
I will continue to spread encouragement to your children, I promise to never quit.

9/15/00

I Call On You

Sometimes, I forget
To seek your kingdom first,
Until I am about to quit
Because I have suffered the worst.
Then there are times, I know
There is no other source of salvation.
I go to You for strength & you show
Guidance, you offer without hesitation.
Please forgive me, I am tragically human
Forever to err & transgress.
No matter what state I find myself in
You give me a home, a place to rest.
Through my joy & also my sorrow
In You I can begin anew.
You open my eyes to another tomorrow
Only You are All Mighty, I call on You.

8/6/01

A New Love Song

Crescendos of laughter & no misery is known,
Tenderness is the melody & at all times respect is shown.
The back-beat is loyalty because integrity is the bass,
Here come the strings of compassion for all in the human race.

Let's write a new love song

No room for profanity because the lyrics are righteously laid,
The singers sing like angels & with joy they are paid.
Altos, Sopranos, Baritones, & Tenors all easily find harmony,
The chorus is healing to all living things, it can make the blind to see.

We are writing a new love song

So you say you cannot read music but I say you can,
My friend these notes can be interpreted by every man.
All you need is a warm heart & an open mind,
& the world's greatest composition you find.

Try writing a new love song

The fearful will suddenly have confidence,
Those who love will never know ill consequence.
Because there is no pain given in exchange for caring,
The selfish will become generous & discover the art of sharing.

Change is in our new love song

3/18/01

Ardd (Earth)

Erde, Gaia

God separated me from the heavens
Forever I am an integral part
Of all that is wondrous
I am from which man was formed
To me he must return.

Erthos, Terre

Rotating, orbiting, maintained by the infinite
Close your eyes, can you feel me?
Warring with my own self
Constantly creating, destroying & recreating
Wounds bearing witness to sins against me.

Masse, Tierra

I am that which is inescapable
Eternally I yield seeds planted
Both righteous & evil reap their rewards
Demanding respect & punishing ungrateful tenants
Inspiring awe & humbling the arrogant
Yet providing solace for the most reverent

& God saw that I was good.

7/4/01

Pyramid Building

The pyramids of old were built on the backs of slaves
During these times some were just emerging from caves
They were built to house the souls of deceased royalty
Or to pay homage to the gods, to bless the crops or calm the sea
I am building my own glorious mansion, my own pyramid
Selfishly tempted to not share, but alas it is too magnificent to be hid.

As history shows the original pyramids were pillaged & plundered
Or were destroyed due to barbaric ignorance, tumbling down with thunder
These pyramids of the ancient represented advanced science & technology
They also demonstrated an advanced philosophy & complex theology
I hope to never again know such hate & not be disgraced
& I am careful that my achievements will not be erased.

So I have laboriously laid the foundation with all the wisdom I am gifted
Making sure that each stone is of the finest material & not easily lifted
I ingeniously mastermind the tunnels & chambers that lay secreted away
I am sure to add all of the luxuries that I desire because here I will forever stay
Fore you see that I am building a pyramid of life & not one for death
It is one to house my spirit & all that is good, not one for material wealth.

It is my sanctuary where I quietly revel in the marvels of this universe
This pyramid is where I rejuvenate my soul & allow my mind to rest
It is my fortress that protects me from all evil & its forces
A place where I return happily & peacefully make my life choices
I openly share this beautiful place with all that are worthy
But this place is for I & I alone, custom made just for me.

It takes several lifetimes to build such a thing that I describe
& many more to fathom this genius & another to keep it alive
By no means have I gotten to the peak of this phenomenal dwelling
But I am almost there & already I feel the power, the energy swelling
All around me is God & His grace is allowing such a project
Arduously I build on, & pray for Him my treasure to protect.

5/8/01

The Truth of The Matter

The truth of the matter is that there is no truth in the matter
People are afraid of dealing with the truth - it shatters
Because at the heart of things the truth is somewhere in their fear
So we run, hide & lie when the truth draws near.

The beauty of it is that no matter where you go it is always there
Challenging & confronting the illusions, pursuing you everywhere
So there is no rest & comfort for the faint of heart
Truth comes down like a tidal wave & will never depart.

> Be glorious & strong in the truth
> Honesty may sting, but it is nothing to dispute
> Let integrity be the foundation & your guiding light
> Allow love to be the judge of your wrong or right

What is repulsive is that truth is just what you believe it to be
Please be prudent in your outlook fore only that you will see
Your lowest & darkest reality will become truth for you
It will become manifest in all that you say & do.

So while you are running & hiding from what is inescapable
I hope you find that you are fallible & yet still capable
Far too many people are moving from one disaster to another
Not taking a good look at themselves, but blaming others.

> Be glorious & strong in the truth
> Honesty may sting, but it is nothing to dispute
> Let integrity be a wind & your guiding light
> Allow love to be the judge of your wrong or right

The truth of the matter is that there is only truth in the matter.

3/22/01

What Do I Know?

The more you know
The more you want to return
Return to blissful ignorance
That once was, that kept you safe
Not safe from physical harm
But safe from corruption
That can spoil the fruitful soul.

What do I know?
       That we have choices & take action daily,
       Even if that action is none at all.

       That love is always the way,
       But is rarely chosen or given - freely.

       That we want, desire & hunger,
       But there is little we truly need.

       That everyone has a purpose & a higher potential,
       But not everyone has the courage to live up to it.

       That art, in all forms, is beautiful,
       But art is individual.

       We are blessed if we love our work,
       But the world is benefited if we are doing our life's work.

       We should do unto others as we have them do unto us,
       But we cannot love another unless we love ourselves.

       God is real!
       It is every person's responsibility to know that Being themselves.

The more you know
The more you thirst
Thirsty not only for knowledge
An insatiable craving for wisdom
There is no more desire for the inane
The hunger becomes constant for understanding
The more I know
I realize, there is so much more to know.

7/8/01

POLITICAL BRAVADO

"I shall allow no man to belittle my soul by making me hate him."
-Booker T. Washington

Caught Up in the Rapture

People always talkin' about there ain't no Black on Black love.
That's not what I see, or is it just my interpretation?
I just can't believe we are that self-loathing, no it couldn't be.
     So I made a list:
Niggas love basketball, Niggas love their cars,
Niggas love collard greens yall, Niggas love their bars.
Now Niggas love to fuck, Niggas love to party & get high,
Niggas love to gamble & the quick buck, Niggas love just gettin by.
Niggas love to...Niggas love you...Niggas love too.
But wait, wasn't the question what do Blacks do?

I always hear people bringin' "You my nigga right?"
What I think they are really sayin' "That don't mean we tight."

People always sayin' that what we need is unity.
We got that down already or is it my imagination?
I can't conceive, my opinion I'm imposing, naw couldn't be.
     So I made a list:
Niggas unite for talk shows, Niggas unite to march,
Niggas unite to smoke blow, Niggas unite but never really start,
Niggas unite to riot & loot, Niggas unite to slang drugs,
Niggas unite to fight & shoot, Niggas unite for gossip & sling mud.
Niggas unite for war...Niggas unite to war...Niggas unite to make war.
But wait, wasn't the question what do Blacks unite for?

I'm always hearin' people sayin' "You my nigga right?"
What I think they are sayin' "I'll stab you in the back tonight".

I am constantly hearin' about honor & respect.
We already do that, I say this without hesitation.
I can't deceive, or was I napping, it just couldn't be.
     So I made a list:
Niggas respect the rich & famous, Niggas respect the pusher & pimp,
Niggas respect who ever can tame us, Niggas respect that fire ass hemp,
Niggas respect the man - you can't deny, Niggas respect the almighty dollar,
Niggas respect the hustle & the lie, Niggas respect the gangbangin' scholar,
Niggas respect game...Niggas respect playin' the game...Niggas respect the game.
But wait, Black men & Niggas ain't one in the same.

CHERYL S. SMITH

I always hear people sayin' "You my nigga right?"
What I think they are sayin' "I have eyes but have no sight."

There's some magic yeah & some Bull Shit too.
Rarely are we shown more than what stereotypes do.
We sometimes have flavor, grace & allure,
We caught up ya'll, but it ain't no rapture.

1999

That Word

We try to convince others that we are still kings & queens,
But we address each other as bitch & all types of disrespect.
The issue is deeper than it seems
We get together & Miriam Webster we check.

Do not define that word,
No matter what you heard,
We are greater & much bigger,
Than NIGGER.

1999

Didn't Know, Then

He hated that he couldn't prosper & get ahead.
He became bitter, full of hate & rage.
He didn't know, then, the truth he did study,
He prayed for wisdom, & unlocked his mental cage.
He pulled up his consciousness in the knick of time,
His saggin' pants were a reflection of his saggin' mind.
He is becoming a man, self-respect he now understands.

Where do I begin,
    Thank you Father
    Because I know now,
What I did not then.

She lamented & believed she would not find a good man,
So she settled for less from every brother.
She didn't know, then, she found decency,
Self-love was required before she could love another.
Started being real with self, low & behold,
She found righteousness or so I am told.
She is taking her place upon a throne, her prince has come along.

Where do I begin,
    Thank you Father
    Because I know now,
What I did not then.

Now there is a lot I still don't know.
Hindsight has given me 20/20 vision.
If I knew then with God leading my life,
I could have slain all evil with precision.
Experience has given me treasures that last
It is all based on what I've learned from the past.
I am learning & growing, constantly improved by just knowing.

Where do I begin,
      Thank you Father
      Because I know now,
What I did not then.

1999

CHERYL S. SMITH

I Don't Have To Care

"I don't have to care"
Were the words from your mouth.
All I could do was stop & stare
You made it plain what you were about.

    Somebody has your ego on ten
    & now you think you don't have to bother.
    To be good to others, both women & men
    But you will answer for that to the Father.

You see life has a way of taking us 180 degrees
& You have to face those you hurt in your past.
Maybe not directly, but you will surely know some unease
Somewhere it says "the last shall be first, & the first will be last".

    Oh the nerve of you to treat someone so cruel!
    No one deserves to know such callousness.
    Don't you know that you are breaking a universal rule?
    Do onto others, as you would have them treat self.

I want to smack you back into reality!
& make you feel my indignation.
I want to make you really see
I'd put you in my shoes without hesitation.

    Remember that everyone is worthy of some respect
    Unless they show you otherwise
    If you are not careful you will not like what you get,
    If you don't bring that ego down a size.

Don't you know better, how did you get this way?
Didn't your mama raise you right?
What in the world would make you even say,
"I don't have to care", yo' shit ain't that tight.

    As you see it you are just telling me what you feel
    & exactly the way it is.
    You are just trying to keep it real
    You don't comprehend "the what goes around, comes around" biz

After it is all said & done
Your attitude is scary & daring.
I hope you can see that everyone
Is worthy of some compassion & caring.

      But even if you don't get it now,
      & my anger you don't understand,
      Your ignorance I will allow,
      Just get back to me when you become a man.

9/25/00

CHERYL S. SMITH

Strange Times

I'm telling you we are experiencing some strange times,
Man, if you let it, these days will blow your mind.

Children are slaughtering one another,
       An automatic weapon is the favorite tool.
Violence was once common only in the inner city,
       But the epidemic has reached the suburban school.
None is safe; no one is exempt from harm.
Warfare reaches from the playground to the family farm.

What insanity is this when convenience is the norm,
       The family meal is prepared in a microwave.
We save boatloads of time & energy,
       But the sit down discussions we do not save.
Mothers & fathers do not show or demand respect.
So how in the world do values & morals we protect?

Don't you find it strange & even surreal,
       That we know so much about our politicians & stars?
Isn't it a shame that so much is known,
       But important information is a mystery, like where your kids are.
I don't care to know about who is sleeping with who.
Stories about real life solutions are far too few.

What about the state of our economy,
       Stocks are falling & many are losing jobs.
But there is a minority that is making millions on the backs of others,
       & don't have the decency to face the hungry & angry mobs.
The government is corrupt & no one works for the common good end.
The working class can only find foes, & sorely needs an influential friend.

I could go on & on about pollution & the cost of fuel,
       Foolishly we are spending billions to send people into space.
Yet there are literally millions who cannot read or eat,
       & thousands more children who know no safe place.
There are still men & women who are being publicly executed.
With these barbaric behaviors the idea of peace is obscure & convoluted.

These issues are just at the tip of an enormous iceberg,
       I have only skimmed the surface of all that is.
But I swear to you that things will only get worse,
       If we don't clean up our act & get down to biz.
It is not someone else's job & no one else's problem to solve.
It takes everyone's effort to progress, & all are involved.

I'm telling you we are experiencing some strange times,
Man, if you let it, these days will blow your mind.

6/5/01

Homicide in Progress

SOMEBODY CALL THE POLICE!
Murder in progress.
Gotten so bad I can't get any rest.
Damn near impossible to find peace.

My job wants all my time & effort.
My family needs my attention & care.
Then it is the daily rat race that is always there.
Call the cops! I want to file a report.

I am only one person. Lone & solitary woman.
I am criticized for being too strong.
Dealt a life to manage on my own.
Inextricable responsibilities, simply doing the best I can.

When will it end? Are they really trying to kill me?
Is there anyone immune from all the insanity?
How do I keep going? What should my next step be?
I swear I can't take the pressure. Got me wanting to flee.

They are killing me silently & softly.
But I am not going down without a fight.
That's why I sleep with my big gun at night.
My weapon of choice is the God within me.

So somebody...anybody...
CALL THE POLICE!
Damn near impossible...
PEACE.

8/8/01

PERSONAL COMPOSITIONS

"All the masterpieces of art contain both light and shadow. A happy life is not one filled with only sunshine, but one which uses both light and shadow to produce beauty."

-Billy Graham

Too Much Woman

5'2", bedroom eyes a soft ruddy brown
Fiery locks I wear as my crown
Shapely lips and curves to match
Simpletons hate and say "she ain't all that"

But baaabbby I am too much woman

I mean it ain't because I am wealthy
It ain't because I stay reasonably healthy
Shit I ain't even the finest thing walkin'
But I demand respect and you will hear me talkin'

Honey I am telling you I am too much woman

I pray to God each and every day
That I don't hurt nobody, but my nerves the evil fray
Just the way some treat others gets me hot
All this man against man shit just has to stop

Don't they know I am too much woman

I can hit the flo' running and not stop until all is done
I can make the moon pale and shame the sun
I have carried more people than Atlas
And I warn you my patience you bet not test

I keep tryin' to tell you I am too much woman

So you think I am insane, you ain't seen nothing yet
Just try messin' with me and mine, all of hell won't take that bet
For if God is for me who can stand against me
Try me and you will know the damage that can be

Stand back 'cause I am too much woman

I am not the kind that is loud and boastful
But if you ask I will offer you no bull
You see it took a long time for me to realize
That it is not always age, but the experience that makes one wise

Hear me now, I am too much woman

A sort of a scholar
A lover that will make you holler
A mother and fine provider
A friend who will lift your spirit higher

The truth is I am too much woman

Too much for whom you say
I am too much for most in every way
The average, the weak and inferior
Get my compassion. Some just don't know they are superior

All little girls should be taught they are too much woman

I was told a long time ago by an elderly star
That you are what you think you are
Damn I wish I understood it then because it took too long
Here I sing my own praise & not someone else's song

I know, I am TOO MUCH WOMAN!

12/28/00

Noisy Ghosts

Oh look at you, you just a fat little girl.
& You kinda cute,
You smart; someday you can rule the world.

You kids are so damn bad and lazy.
You can't even clean right,
You and your brother drove your mother crazy.

*Voices inside my head
Echoes words that you said*

Your own father won't even take care of you.
You are worthless and fast,
I can't wait until you turn eighteen so I can be through.

Come here little girl, yea you with the big ass.
Must be jelly 'cause jam don't shake like that,
What! You only 12, you got more than you should have.

*Voices inside my head
Echoes words that you said*

You would do this if you care about me.
If I leave you will be nothing,
You ain't shit anyway, I just wanted to fuck and now I'll flee.

Boy you sholl do talk real proper.
So what, you grew up around white peoples,
I guess she think she's better, says she gon be a doctor.

*Voices inside my head
Echoes words that you said*

You kinda' cute…
You smart though…
You don't act like a fat girl…
You have to give mo…
What makes you think he really likes you…
You can't trust a man as far as you can throw them…
You get out of life all you deserve…
Girl, no she ain't trying to get with him…

Voices inside my head
Echoes words that you said

Bitch if you tell I will kill you.
You shouldn't have been acting like that,
I won't let him see me cry and do what I must do.
Somewhere I learned that I am unworthy of love and respect.
Except for using my brain, the three R's got me through.

He didn't know that I could never confess his sin
I can't ever admit that I brought on such shame.
Oh God I want to start over, find somewhere else to begin.
I will never be able to tell that dirty secret, I cannot give it a name.

Voices inside my head
Echoes words that you said

So I walk around normal,
I try not to let people see the real me,
I pretend not to be fat and obscene.
I try to comfort the girl that is ungrateful and unworthy.

The tears come pouring out, for all that was lost.
I am full of sorrow for the beautiful girl slain and the ruthless lie.
No child should know what I have known.
& I pray that not another is ever visited by…

Voices inside my head
Echoes words that you said

11/6/00

---

* Inspired by Voices Inside my Head; written, arranged, performed by Sting.

My Amira - My Princess

Beautiful almond shaped eyes
Your soul glimmers through them when you smile.
Your laughter resonates & rebuilds my spirit,
I just watch you play, dance & sing for awhile.

I am prayerful always for your safety & your peace,
You are growing too fast & I sometimes marvel.
You keep me striving to be better than my best,
I am forever cautious, & careful to keep you well.

I praise God for your health & that I can be your mother,
I am grateful for the time we have together to share.
You make this world a wonderful place to just be,
For no other I can love more, always know that I will be there.

The world I delivered you into can be cruel at times,
But I will try to shield you from all its wickedness.
To rock you in my arms & provide you a safe haven,
My gift, my Amira, because of you I am blessed.

3/19/01

Beloved Daughter

From the beginning I have failed you
Not ensuring you an equal footing
I chose incorrectly a boy
Too weak to be a man
Your father.

My beloved & precious girl
I try to make amends
By doing twice the work
Too strong to give up being
Your mother.

In years to come
I hope you will understand
That you gave me
Purpose in an absurd world
My dearest daughter.

8/6/01

Sista' Friends

I want to introduce you to some powerful friends of mine,
They are all awesome & phenomenal women of their time.
Their beauty is incomparable, each with unique talents & gifts,
Every one of them possesses the ability to sooth, inform & uplift.

I will start with her that I have known too many years, let's not count,
She is a light chocolate beauty queen, but her wit you cannot surmount.
She is fearless & ain't afraid to reach for the highest of peaks,
Svelte in stature & believe me she'll charm you when she speaks.

Next comes the sassy & amusing reddish brown honey,
Inside her is a ball of energy that she quickly spends like money.
She is mothering, but not overbearing, forever being helpful,
Short sexy brown sugar is the package, never once being boastful.

Please welcome the chili pepper of the bunch, adding spice to my days,
She is often fiery & saucy, & I admire her motivating ways.
Over a short period of time she & I have become a perfect fit,
Don't underestimate my fair & beautiful Puerto Rican Lil Bit.

Lastly, I want to mention one of the newest members of the group,
She is calming & has a healing spirit like that of chicken soup.
She is a soldier for Christ, & the gospel she is eager to share,
Cafe-au-lait, she'll shame most fashion models with her fanciful air.

I feel at home with these goddesses & turn to them when in need,
I have cried on their shoulders, & my soul they all feed.
I strive to reciprocate every ounce of what they all provide,
I realize that I am wealthy & strong with these women at my side.

I am not promised to see another God blessed day,
So I will take this public opportunity to say,
Gina, Sharon, Maritza & Angela you are my Sista' friend,
Thank you for all you bestow, your inspiration has no end.

3/27/01

Hey Girl, I miss you

Hey girl! How ya' doin'
I pray that everything is well
We have so much to share
So many new secrets to tell.

It's been too long
& I don't remember what went wrong
Why we stopped speaking
But know I care & now you I am seeking.

I'm seeking you out
To make sure you are fine
I want you to know
You are constantly on my mind.

Has too much time passed
Jeeze times moves much too fast
I hear you are happy
How are you & the family?

We had been friends since childhood
Turning to each other for support
Sharing most things, the bad & good
& we couldn't wait to talk, for the next report.

I remember those days, bittersweet
Adolescent summers of heat
Adult autumns of change
Now we are our parents, don't it seem strange?

Remember when we dreamed about now
We weren't in a hurry to get here
I think we wanted our independence
But our youth & the good times were dear.

Back then I was not mature enough
To always tell the important stuff
You were appreciated & I still care
You were my friend & were always there.

May God smile on you
& on all you have chosen to do
All the blessings He will bestow
I pray that only love you will ever know.

Whatever the reason for our parting
The drama of another world
I just wanted to let you know
I really miss you girl.

7/22/01

My Muse

Thank you for loving me.
Love aligns me with my gift
That powerful energy that awakens
That allows my tired eyes to clearly see.

Thank you for hating me.
Hate challenges my muscles
That cowardice of all energy
Laying wait in lies & hustles.

Thank you for sharing.
All that you were suppose to give
Putting yourself at risk
So a soul like mine continues to live.

Thank you for taking.
All that you require from me
Reinforcing the idea that everything cost
Nothing is ever truly free.

There isn't much in between love & hate.
You either give or you take
Any way you choose
Unwittingly you have been my muse.

5/8/01

Mentally Broken

Over the years I have
Heard
Saw
Felt
Experienced
Your story
But I was not there for it all.

Over the years I have
Listened
Witnessed
Survived
Lived
Your story
Now I testify to your fall.

Listening to the stories of your youth
You grew up poor, but rich in your religion
A religion that stifled, & kept you in line
But one that did not always tell you the truth.

Did it speak the truth of your grandeur & ultimate potential?
Did it tell of how power & strength was yours
Yours to possess, & necessary for survival
Or was it one that told you the lie that happiness was incidental?

Over the years I have listened to the tales of your goodness
That goodness described as quiet & obedient
The eldest sister who was kind to her siblings, cooked & cleaned
But what of the girl who knew rape? Mother that was not your sin to confess.

What become of that girl when it was all too hard to bear?
When the reality of what you suffered through was too painful
Where did you turn, where could you run
Who could help you, when you needed someone to be there?

I had the pleasure to witness greatness. The mother I once knew
One who remains continually gentle & compassionate
Forever patient with her grandchildren
But what of the wife, when her husband was through?

When he beat you, & snorted up every last dime
My brother & I watching, wanting to stop that madness
How you fought valiantly for yours - our - survival
When you decided this would be the very last time.

We were witnesses to your working from dusk till dawn
Often times from dawn to whenever
Leaving us with friends & neighbors to keep us safe
Exhausted & fatigued but forever concerned about the damn lawn.

Always concerned about what the outside folks would say
But never giving yourself the same amount of concern
Know that I appreciate that you worked double & triple shifts
Just to make sure we had food, assuring us there was a way.

We survived as a family for awhile - well...until
Until you could be alone no more as a woman
So you sought a mate, a father & someone to lighten the load
That is when you introduced the demon, known simply as Bill.

In waltzed that man & I suppose he was only what he knew
But he was foreigner & a stranger, alien I suppose
Because he offered nothing but turmoil & unrest
This is when I remember your insanity became manifest, when it grew.

We lived with that creature, one who lied & abused his way
Into our lives & made our beautiful lakefront home
Into a huge shack, a place of torture & shame
Tearfully I remember that home, memory bittersweet to this day.

We survived because of your blood, sweat & tears
I guess that is why I continue to strive, this is why I fight on
Because of all that you were able to maintain
Clearly, I remember your love & how it fed us in those lean years.

That house was not the issue & was never really important
It is what was nurtured & built before Bill's arrival
Your family, our family, that was established
That which he destroyed, the bonds that were so magnificent.

Your story is one of beauty & I am sorry if I do not covey
That my mother is & will always be a fantastic woman to know
Although her physical beauty is fading, outwardly she is weathered
You can hear her beautiful voice speaking through all I have to say.

I am the daughter of a woman who is mentally shattered & broken
Society is most fond of the term crazy or comfortable with mentally ill
But her ease is not found in a potion & neither is it in a pill
It was abandoned in neglected expression, in words that remain unspoken.

Mother, there is so much that I am incapable of knowing
About your life & your world, & some things I will never understand
But I pay homage to the woman who did the best she could
It is because of your love & your beauty we are reproducing.

Producing new & improved children who I will be able to tell this tale
But children who will have it better than us, that is as it should be
Precious ones who will for generations & throughout the years
Hear, see, feel but never experience your story & know that all is well.

7/10/01

Reincarnate

A thousand times I see you
Walking in & out of my life
Different forms but for the same reasons
Complicated things of strife.

A million times I have kissed you
Hungers satisfied & thirst quenched
However only momentarily
Happiness sought & often felt.

For an eternity I have known you
Only to say farewell, but never good bye
We will never be apart for long
Destiny offers no fable, conjures no lie.

So easily we fall out of each other's lives
Only to return to learn what we do not know
Every time carrying away knowledge
If we do not struggle against it we will grow.

What is it this time that we are seeking
What message do we have for the other
In what way are we enriched by the experience
Have we pleased fate this life or must there be another?

I am conscious this time around in this cycle
That you are my familiar & forever have been
Now I humbly ask how can I help you
My lover, daughter, brother, father, mother & friend.

All of you have walked with me in another life
How can I assist you in your ascension
In what way do I play a role in your enlightenment
How can I help you reach another dimension?

How long or short our paths will cross is unknown
It is not me that created things as they are
But I am one of the forces that influences all events
I have the power to move mountains & to create stars.

Each of us has the ability to divine miracles
We were created in His own image & likeness
Because of this we have insurmountable strength
If we can tap into a fraction of it, we are blessed.

A thousand times I have loved you
Salutations a millions times more
Eternally I will know you
Until we truly get what we came here for.

5/8/01

I See You

Siting at my window I watch you hustle,
  Braids in your hair
   Saggin' pants reveal your underwear
You move your work - a 24-hour bustle.

Son, I see you

Parked on a bench near downtown,
  Hair cut close to your head
   WallStreet & EM signal that you maybe well read
I can feel your heavy spirit & on your face a frown.

Brother, I see you

Perched on a stool at the local bar,
  Ball cap propped on your top
   Uniform shirt, collar unbuttoned & the sleeves you crop
You drink one after another dreaming of someplace far.

Father, I see you

Unwinding at a coffee shop sitting to the side,
  Dreadlocks hidden under a wrap
   Free flowing cotton & carrying a messenger bag,
The caffeine a pick-me-up, dog tired after a long ride.

Provider, I see you

Pent behind a desk, I'm stuck in my box,
  Afro nicely shaped after a bi-weekly cut
   Reports stuffed under arm, you don't just walk you strut
Your charisma is envied, but you are trusted like a fox.

Friend, I see you

Whatever walk of life,
      No matter where you are going
      No matter what you are longing
I am your mother, sister, daughter, companion, goddess, & your wife.

God, I see you

3/18/01

CHERYL S. SMITH

Mama, Across the Street

I see you almost everyday,
Just sitting
I wonder if there is a way,
Just wishing
I could ease your daily load,
Just watching
Your tragedy unfold,
Just praying
The grand kids left for you to raise,
Just hoping
That you will soon come out of your daze,
Just sitting.

8/6/01

Sky Scraping

Full metal jackets,
all colors
shapes & sizes.
Standing side by side
Towering
Lone in granduer
Looking down
always reaching up
towards heaven.

Windows never open
peering out, vantage point
unique observations.
Believing
Always exposed to peril
Unceasingly toiling
always growing
towards heaven.

See the clouds
of dreams floating
over your dome.
You are magnificent
Striving
Accompanied by like kind
Soaring upward
always striving
towards heaven.

8/11/01

LOVE'S TEMPO

"Let no one come to you without leaving better and happier."
-Mother Teresa

In The Dance

The rhythm had me, the cadence of your words
The beat of our attraction is all I heard,
"Here comes the boom, here comes the boom"
There is imminent danger, but no certain doom
In The Dance

The dance was between two for the world to see
You could feel the eyes full of spite & pure envy
"Shake your ass, watch yourself"
Because there is only you & I & no one else
In The Dance

I felt the power of the bass & the beauty of the treble
We entice & excite & find passion at new levels
"No, No, you don't love me & I know now"
But passion is to be shown, let me show you how
In The Dance

It was never said, but neither wanted an end
Could you, my dance partner, become my friend
"Gotta keep on, gotta keep on, searchin to find the one"
We wouldn't stop until it was done
In The Dance

The beat is steady & pulsing with power
The melody drifted on, as rainbow dreams came in a shower
"Love rain down on me, down on me"
Is this where things are left & should be
In The Dance

We left the joint still rapturous & in the mood
We were famished, but craved for more than food
"Do, do, do, do, all that I can say"
We danced on & on until the sun rose & produced a new day
In The Dance

I hope all can experience & have the chance to enjoy
The first time between girl & boy
"Let's make it last forever & forever"
That we as partners endeavor
In The Dance

9/20/00

Bermuda Moon

Laying in the pale sand
With you next to me.
Caribbean stranger holding my hand
I could stay this way a century,
Under this beautiful Bermuda moon.

The waves crashing to the shore
While we explore one another.
This moment in time can offer no more
Taking us up to & no farther,
A visit to a gorgeous Bermuda moon.

Soft fragrant breezes full of delight
Solitude under the stars.
I reach out to you on this night
I am Venus & you are Mars,
Paying homage to the Bermuda moon.

I am humbled by this splendid scene
All around is God & this is His domain.
We rest peacefully & serene
I can never be the same,
I made love under a Bermuda moon.

8/6/01

CHERYL S. SMITH

I Wanted You to Say My Name

12 am
Blustery snowy night
Hurrying to warmth
Running to find what is right.

I imagine the whispers in your baritone
Oh to hear the bass in your prolonged moan.

I arrive & you greet with silence,
There are no inquiries regarding my day, my week, my life.
I ignore the chill as I enter your residence,
Secretly I try to exorcise the demons of our strife.

The gentle familiar or your countenance,
I long to cross your barrier, to disable your defense.

You just lay there waiting, or are you thinking,
I am impatient, but try not to disrupt your mood.
So I take a seat at your side,
As you remain quiet & begin to brood.

Gently my mind swoons with every moment that passes,
I see this insanity & that it is burning to ashes.

I am aware that you will make no motions,
So I remind you that my time will come to an end.
I request that we partake in a love potion,
I pretend it is something medicinal that is shared between friends.

The reality of the situation is shown as we dress the bed,
No courtesy is given & no protest is said.

Within I hear loves songs which is opposite of what is to follow,
You provide underground Hip Hop, I suppose that is your preference.
I make no more assumptions & accept that this thing is hollow,
I make my inner love & strength my point of reference.

My inner being sees the light of intimacy,
In your arms I am content to just be.

Then comes the time to receive what I came to get,
Precious reminders are your caresses & tenderly you deliver.
As you rub my body you erase cruel times spent,
Completely I give into the ride, & totally I surrender.

Diligently I worked my body to please,
You provided the rhythm deftly & with ease.

Please say sweet nothings to repair my compromised will,
Tell me how much you want to heal my scarred heart.
Speak of my beauty - the beauty that is I still,
Say my name & allow us to gain a new start.

I wanted you to supernaturally read my brain,
You could have made me whole by just saying my name.

So together we slowly ebb & flow like tides one upon another,
But like oil & water we touch but can never mix.
I will always care for you like a brother & crave for you my lover,
But my passion for you is tragically an incomplete fix.

You work with eyes closed & lips sealed tight,
I am convinced now that you are on a secret voyage - a personal flight.

I wearily rise from your side unable to put my yearning to rest,
Dreaming, wishing & praying that you were a place I could stay.
My mind still cloudy with alcohol yet my soul still heavy with consciousness,
Too aware that our parting could be forever as we face another day.

For you & me - the we that never materialized,
I weep silently for what has been realized.

My tears are not out of regret,
Our lessons to one another were fundamental.
What we wanted the universe couldn't yield just yet,
I will forever be grateful that you were kind & gentle.

My unspoken request was so simple & plain,
I just wanted you to say my name.

CHERYL S. SMITH

3 am
Blustery snowy morn
Running away from what was
Hurrying to someplace warm.

3/17/01

Tonight

Tonight, I needed the man
A man with whom I can commune.
Someone who'll listen to the unspoken
A man who is in touch, one in tune.

Tonight, I wanted the man
A man I could be held by.
Someone who would caress my mind
A man not always knowing, but willing to try.

Tonight, I prayed for the man
A man I could dream about tomorrow.
One who would erase my painful yesterday
A man who will bring joys & never sorrows.

Tonight, I need the man
But that puzzle remains unsolved.
Tonight I still have that want & prayer
Because tonight no man ever called.

7/25/01

Momentary Friend

Hey did you hear the news
I took a gamble & did not lose.
What in the world you say
I made a new friend today.

Well he & I aren't really new
It's just I was slow to see.
I mean I felt his spirit all the while
I just didn't know how he saw me.

I shared with this special being
Something precious, something not to be discarded.
They returned the favor triple fold
& then we kissed farewell & I departed.

How could it be that I walked away so easily
How is it that I can go on so busily.
When will I return & revisit this friend
That is uncertain because this could be the end.

You see my new friend & I shared a moment
A designated time in a world of the infinite.
We exchanged joys that neither will forget
& then made no promise & no remorse is found in it.

I wanted to talk, but instead I listened
I heard the prophecy of greatness.
I wanted to run from the fire of that mind
Instead I stood in awe & wondered "who designed this?"

This person so inspired & full of light
One who cannot idle, unless they expire.
This gentle soul that is willing to fight for the right
I pray for their wisdom to rest when they tire.

It sounds trite but he enriched my mind
This Angel in human form did I find.
Who washed my body & fortified my soul
I will remember this day when I am ancient & old.

Should I be so fortunate to share another time
To experience the ecstasy that was mine.
I will revel in the euphoria & give all I can
I look forward to sharing & partaking again.

When my friend & I share a moment.

12/00

CHERYL S. SMITH

Can We Try

Life keeps pulling us in different directions.
At times I don't know whether I've arrived or I'm going.
You have your own concerns & obligations.
How do we make time to satisfy our longings?

So many people demanding our attention.
So many things that must be done.
I have my priorities that I won't begin to mention.
Been running so long, surely this race I've won.

We can't seem to get together, what is this?
Something happens or something comes up.
But I need for you to know I miss your kiss.
I dream of our conversations & yearn for your touch.

We have spent years passing up on one another.
Then pausing long enough to reignite love's embers.
Years wasted on stand-bys, but still caring for the other.
Our encounters brief yet deep. Yes, I fondly remember.

Let's stop running from the real.
Both of us guilty of not being ready until today.
We have both grown, & now in tune with how we feel.
Can we build a tomorrow together? Is there a way?

Can we slow down the rotation of the world, & finally join as one?
Can we explore what we have been creating over this lifetime?
Or is it meant that we remain separate? Me a red moon & you a yellow sun.
Is it possible for me to share your bright day & you partake in my dreamy
nighttime?

You see time is short & forever is known by no living man.
I am asking for the truth, there is no need to lie.
If the answer is a negative, I'm mature enough to understand.
Simply answer with a yes or a no. Can we try?

7/24/01

Leaving

Sometimes leaving is the most difficult action that I must take.
I dislike the finality that I feel, and the void farewell can create.
But I have to go…

It doesn't help when you ask me to stay or just wait till morning.
It becomes almost impossible when your affections I am yearning.
You know I have to go…

Nor does it help that I know there are those who are willing to take my place.
There are too many who can happily warm my vacated space.
Yet I still have to go…

Please don't touch me there or say those words I need to hear.
I will remember you fondly when I think that love was so near.
I must go…

Soon you will come to the realization that you no longer want me.
This fact I have already pondered, dealt with and peace I achieve.
And now I must go…

So I will be leaving and I will kiss you this last time Good Bye.
I will turn and walk away fast, take a deep breathe and will not cry.
I have to go…

You will feel some relief and perhaps a bit of sadness.
I should have not stayed as long as I have, but hunger made me linger.
I have been unwise and have neglected my other obligations I confess.
I am sure you want no excuses, to think you didn't really care is the stinger.
So, I must go…

I have considered that this was all a game, and not much more.
Players ain't all the same, but they all have to score.
Knowingly I go…

I have learned my lesson and it is time for me to move on.
A new tune to hum and I'll compose new words to my love song.
I'm gone.

10/26/00

Slave For Time

If I could make time slow to the rhythm of my heart
Each time you walk into the room
The cadence of each tick would slow in measure to half.

If time were mine to command I would tell it never to start
Each time you kiss & touch me there
It would remain idle as you penetrate with your staff.

If I could master the hands on the face of every clock
They would speed to a blinding rate
Every time you desired & lusted after another.

If I conquered space & time I'd keep the secret under lock
There would be no spare key
Every time you decided to take a different lover.

If gluttony & greed are cardinal sins
Then surely my soul will not win.
For I am selfish with your sex
In my passion I am vexed.

The lie is that time has healing power
In your absence I am tortured with every passing hour.

My wishes & dreams are many
But in this one line
I repent my want for tyranny
Over Father Time.

He is my enemy, my foe; I try to be brave
I continue to lose every battle & I remain a slave - for time.

3/2000

This Time

This time I am going to use all of my God given senses
And they are not limited to just five.
Sight, touch, taste, smell and hearing are commonly known,
But it takes more to truly stay alive.

I will keep my eyes wide open to allow myself to really see
Even when I am kissing you and things are moving fast.
I want to make sure I am kissing your lips,
Not unknowingly kissing your ass.

I will allow myself to be touched,
Hopefully you will be gentle with my heart.
But I will not foolishly open up without caution,
Trust must be established in the beginning, at the start.

I will savor the sweet and saltiness that is you,
Fully I recognize that you are just a man.
Patiently I accept the good and the bad,
Unconditional love I pray you can understand.

I will happily snuggle into the scent of you,
But remain conscious to note the first signs of fire.
Through hard-earned wisdom I know how to flee,
When cruelty takes the place of compassion & desire.

I will make sure to truly listen to every word you have to say,
Special care will be given to what remains unsaid.
Most people will tell all that you need to know of them,
I will be prudent - not allow my heart to cloud my head.

Most importantly this time I will use my intuition,
What I favor to name as my God sense.
To avoid the hurt and emptiness that follows unwise decisions
I will let God guide me through, to skip the ill consequence -
      THIS TIME.

6/5/01

CHERYL S. SMITH

I Ain't She

I ain't she
& she ain't me
& I'm tired as hell
Of her memory
Interfering with we!

Every time I turn around I'm cleaning up
Behind some other women's mess she left behind.
I mean putting back together broken brothers
That let some chick scar their hearts & mess up their mind.
It comes back to the same ole shit & I can't catch a break
I'm not sure if it's worth it. Don't know how much mo' I can take.

I ain't she
& she ain't me
& I'm tired as hell
Of her memory
Interfering with we!

What's a girl to do, just admit to defeat
& run away at the first signs of drama?
Should I leave their asses just as I found them
Or send them back home to their mamas?
It comes back to the same ole shit & I can't catch a break
I'm not sure if it's worth it. Don't know how much mo' I can take.

I ain't she
& she ain't me
& I'm tired as hell
Of her memory
Interfering with we!

You are quick to call me the bag lady
But then that would make you the bag man.
Loose the grocery carts of self-pity, anger & hurt
Get over it, move on boy & deal with what's at hand.
It comes back to the same ole shit & I can't catch a break
I'm not sure if it's worth it. Don't know how much mo' I can take.

I ain't she
&
She ain't me!

8/3/01

Tortoise Shell

Planning for wealth & adventuring about
But you never strayed far from your shell.
Your world is burdensome yet secretly you dream
Your shield is heavy but serves you well.

Creating gaily & seducing playfully
I am constantly fluttering to & fro.
My world has no borders so I merrily soar
I am joyous for the miracles I am blessed to know.

We meet on the road of higher learning
Both intrigued by the words we both sing.
Brought together by what was destined
You in your beautiful shell & me in my lovely wings.

So I being me with my aggressive ways
& you with your polished armor standing strong.
Begin to share a bit of what is each of us
But soon you recognized something was wrong.

At last I became too invasive, getting too close too soon
Too late I discovered you prefer a much quieter song.
Suddenly you withdrew to the safety of your shell &
I was left befuddled, trying to decipher what went wrong.

Unwisely I persisted and tried to draw you out
So proud of my beauty, I brilliantly displayed my light.
Adversely you were blinded by my luminescence
I now know my love for you was much too bright.

In spite of the walls you have meticulously laid
I saw & cared for the creature that dwells within.
Gladly I will meet you somewhere in the heavens
Your shell discarded, free to no longer pretend.

Fondly I remember your slow but progressive drag
As always I try to learn from the errors I have made.
I am grateful to you my ambitious & dreamy tortoise friend
Know that the wisdom you gifted will never fade.

3/26/01

Shark Bitten

Swimming along in this school of life,
    I happened upon a Shark.
        He was stealthily cruising along,
            Exchanging his fame for fortune.
I mistook this infamous creature of strife,
    As gentle & like myself a dolphin.
        Not until I was bitten did I know otherwise,
            This is where the good stuff begun.
Together we were learning, working, playing - growing,
    For both of us appreciated how like & unlike we were.
        Independently we accomplished our goals,
            Stronger because we could call on the other.
The Shark & I never knew where the other was going,
    But somehow confident in the other's return.
        Outwardly we were different species,
            But inwardly we shared as sister & brother.
I find myself wondering how I got to know,
    Such a magnificent & dangerous kind.
        Daringly I continued on my trek, which involves him,
            He that spoke to my intellect & communicated with my soul.
Stormy & choppy was our flow,
    But rough seas were easily navigated.
        The hunter & the communicator finding one another,
            Neither the dominant, none having absolute control.
Separately we dive, fly, work - create,
    Infinite are the possibilities of our lives.
        Joyously we live, content to let each just be,
            What the Creator has deemed as good & certain.
Passion was ever prevalent, neither wanted to abate,
    But a Shark will always be a predator.
        & The Dolphin will always be a thinker,
            Both changed forever, because the Dolphin was Shark bitten.

6/13/01

Exhaling the Rhyme

The choices I have made have led me to this point
The black punctuation I have run into
Which I cannot pass until I pause, inhale the joint
& exhale the rhyme that is you.

Black like the night that you dwell in
As beautiful as a bird of a haunted paradise.
You are traveling but no where have you been
Your arms are warm, but your heart is ice.
Your back is strong from carrying horrifying memories
Your mind sharp easily converting weight into cash.
But your spirit is weary from all the terror that it sees
Your morals and your business too often clash.

Jagged are your edges, hard is the image
Misunderstood are your motives.
Witness to your brother's carnage
Exploiting all the here & now gives.
For no future are you planning
But constantly you dream of tomorrow.
The bus of the temporary you are voyaging
Very little love you allow yourself to know.

Knowingly I see the not so apparent
What lies beneath the rough appearance.
Bruised & damage is the content
Openly I love, giving you a chance.
But I hedge my bet on you, aware of your fear
You are crippled by your own insecurity.
Lashing out & wounding those you hold dear
Not because you are cruel, simply because of proximity.

Cautiously you experiment in the science of me
Expecting the whole thing to explode.
In the meantime you set your soul free
Finally able to lay down your cumbersome load.
But trust is too foreign, so you are unable to rest
You have known too much betrayal.
You see me as some sick & twisted test
The truth is that rejecting love is where you fail.

The choices I have made have led me to this point
The black punctuation I have run into
Which I cannot pass until I pause, inhale the joint
I have exhaled the rhyme that is you.

7/4/01

PRAYERFUL FINALE

"Let your religion be less of a theory and more of a love affair."
-G.K. Chesterton

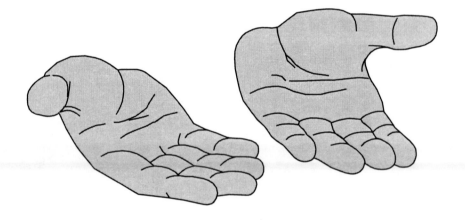

Now I Lay Me Down To Sleep

NOW...

In my quiet place I talk to You Father God.
Reverently, I approach You on Your throne,
Joyfully, I thank you for Your many blessings.
Nothing I accomplish & have is mine alone.
It is through Your grace & mercy that I live!
To You be the glory, & all praises I give!

I LAY...

My burdens at your feet, & ask Your forgiveness.
Humbly, I ask that You wash my soul clean.
Devotedly, I pray for Your guidance & Divine intellect.
I am sure to thank you in advance, for fortune unseen.
It is through Your grace & mercy that I live!
To You be the glory, & all praises I give!

ME...

That I have become is only a fraction of what will be.
Happily, I go through challenges that build my spirit.
Patiently, I wait for You to bring me out.
I know that Your wealth is endless, You never quit.
It is through Your grace & mercy that I live!
To You be the glory, & all praises I give!

DOWN TO SLEEP...

I find peace & tranquility. In You I am renewed.
Peacefully, I slumber under Your omnipresent eye.
Restfully, I rejuvenate for the new day that will come.
I feel serenity because I know You are standing by.
It is through Your grace & mercy that I live!
To You be the glory, & all praises I give!

I PRAY THE LORD, MY SOUL TO KEEP.

7/19/01

ABOUT THE AUTHOR

Cheryl Smith now lives in Chicago, IL.with her 2 year-old daughter and mother. She is presently completing her Professional Studies degree at Roosevelt University and is working full-time as an accounting analyst for The Northern Trust Bank. The following great African American authors encourage and have influenced Cheryl: Margaret Walker, Zora Neale Hurston, Amiri Baraka, Haki Madhubuti, Langston Hughes, Countee Cullen, Myra Viola Wilds, Gwendolyn Brooks, Maya Angelou and Nikki Giovanni. However, the everyday tragic, triumphant, repulsive and splendid things, people and events inspire her to write. Cheryl is currently working on her second book of poetry and short stories.